PRESIDENTS OF THE U.S.A.

Warren G. Harding

Our Twenty-Ninth President

by Gerry and Janet Souter

THE CHILD'S WORLD®

29

The Child's World®

PUBLISHED IN THE UNITED STATES OF AMERICA

THE CHILD'S WORLD®
1980 Lookout Drive • Mankato, MN 56003-1705
800-599-READ • www.childsworld.com

ACKNOWLEDGMENTS
The Child's World®: Mary Berendes, Publishing Director

Creative Spark: Mary McGavic, Project Director; Melissa McDaniel, Editorial Director; Deborah Goodsite, Photo Research

The Design Lab: Kathleen Petelinsek, Design; Gregory Lindholm, Page Production

Content Adviser: David R. Smith, Adjunct Assistant Professor of History, University of Michigan–Ann Arbor

PHOTOS
Cover and page 3: White House Historical Association (White House Collection) (detail); White House Historical Association (White House Collection)

Interior: The Art Archive: 17 (Culver Pictures); Associated Press: 12, 18 and 39, 34; Corbis: 5, 19, 20, 22, 26, 36, 37 (Bettmann), 9, 11, 25, 33, 35 (Corbis), 21 and 39 (David J. & Janice L. Frent Collection), 27 (Schenectady Museum; Hall of Electrical History Foundation); Getty Images: 24 (Topical Press Agency), 29 (Hulton Archive); The Granger Collection, New York: 31; The Image Works: 4 (Roger-Viollet); iStockphoto: 44 (Tim Fan); Library of Congress: 30; Marion County Historical Society, Marion, Ohio: 32; National First Ladies' Library: 13; Ohio Historical Society: 6, 8 and 38, 10, 14 and 38, 15, 16; Picture History: 7; U.S. Air Force photo: 45.

LIBRARY OF CONGRESS CATALOGING-IN-PUBLICATION DATA
Souter, Gerry.
Warren G. Harding / by Gerry and Janet Souter.
p. cm. — (Presidents of the U.S.A.)
Includes bibliographical references and index.
ISBN 978-1-60253-057-7 (library bound : alk. paper)
1. Harding, Warren G. (Warren Gamaliel), 1865–1923—Juvenile literature.
2. Presidents—United States—Biography—Juvenile literature. I. Souter, Janet, 1940– II. Title. III. Series.

E786.S678 2008
973.914092—dc22
[B]

2008002302

Warren G. Harding served as president from 1921 to 1923.

TABLE OF CONTENTS

CHAPTER ONE

BORN TO SUCCEED

Phoebe Dickerson Harding delivered her first-born child at the Harding farm in Corsica, Ohio, on November 2, 1865. (Today, Corsica is called Blooming Grove.) Phoebe and her husband named their child Warren Gamaliel Bancroft Winnipeg Harding. He would be the first of their eight children.

Warren G. Harding in 1921

Warren's father, George Tryon Harding, was a doctor. At the time, many people in America's farming communities had little money. Instead of paying cash, many people traded goods and services with each other. The people of Corsica knew George Harding was willing to trade. He might accept a bag of seed for his medical services. Then he might trade that seed for a shovel at the general store.

Phoebe Harding was also a doctor. She earned her medical license by helping her husband and working

Six-year-old Warren Harding poses with two of his younger sisters. His mother called him "Winnie."

as a midwife, a person who helps deliver babies. Between her work and farm chores, she was busy, but she found time to begin Warren's education while he was still quite young. She was a religious woman and read the Bible to her son. She also taught him poems. Warren was a bright child and could read by age four.

In addition to being a doctor, George Harding taught himself veterinary medicine.

By the time he was a teenager, Warren was tall and handsome. He was also muscular from working on his father's farm. His many friends enjoyed his company, but Warren was also independent. He liked to spend

Warren Harding's mother, Phoebe, was strong-willed and loving. She wanted the best for her son and started his reading lessons when he was still very young.

time by himself. In addition to working on his father's farm, young Warren helped build fences for his neighbors. He also worked for the Toledo & Ohio Railroad, helping to lay track.

George Harding wanted to help his son in any way he could. He gave Warren a small piece of land to farm. Warren could sell his crops to earn extra money. Then George Harding became part owner of a newspaper. Warren took a job at the paper as the "printer's devil." This meant he did odd jobs around the office.

He swept up, cleaned ink off the print machines, ran errands, and learned about the business of running a small weekly newspaper.

Even with his busy work schedule, Warren liked having a good time. He enjoyed music and learned to play a horn. Then he and his friends started a band. Warren's outgoing nature and good looks made him popular. The band allowed him to travel throughout the area, making more friends along the way.

In 1879, at age 14, Warren entered tiny Ohio Central College to study with its faculty of 12 instructors. He became the editor of the school newspaper, called *The Ohio Central College Journal of Knowledge and Josh*. (*Josh* is another word for "joke.") This gave

Warren Harding was born in this house in Corsica, Ohio.

Warren the chance to have his writing published for the first time. In the summer, he painted barns for $25 each, including the paint. He used the money to help pay for his schooling. It seemed like everything was going well for hardworking Warren Harding. His life was on the right track.

While still a teenager, Harding graduated from college. He then passed the Ohio state teaching exam. He tried teaching but didn't like it. Then he tried selling insurance, but he didn't like that either. When his family moved to Marion, Ohio, in 1882, Harding took a job with the *Marion Democratic Mirror* newspaper as a writer—and a floor sweeper.

Harding was known as an excellent speaker. He had a beautiful voice and liked to talk to the public. His warmth made audiences believe that he truly cared about them.

Warren graduated from Ohio Central College when he was just 16 years old. He then became a teacher. Eventually, he decided to pursue a newspaper career.

The offices of the Marion Star *were in this building. Harding owned the paper from 1884 to 1923.*

Harding's career at the *Mirror* was brief. The Hardings were **Republicans,** but the *Mirror*'s editor was a staunch **Democrat.** People from the two **political parties** often had differences of opinion. In 1884, the Republicans **nominated** James G. Blaine as their presidential **candidate.** He ran against the Democratic candidate, Grover Cleveland. Harding went to a political **rally** for Blaine and returned to work wearing a paper hat with a Blaine ribbon attached. The editor fired him on the spot.

Harding was not out of the newspaper business for long. Two of his friends heard that the *Marion Star,* a small newspaper in Marion, was for sale. They suggested that the three of them pool their money and buy it for $300. Harding had always liked **journalism.** He put in his share of the money and became part owner of the newspaper at age 19.

Over the next five years, Warren Harding learned every part of the newspaper business, from setting type to deciding what stories the newspaper would print. Later, he became the sole owner of the *Marion Star*. He became an important member of the community, respected by the townspeople. He established his own **creed** for his paper that told its employees what was expected of them. Harding wanted to run his paper with honesty and integrity. He hated **sensational** articles that lured readers with stories of crime, tragedy, and misfortune. Part of his creed stated: "There's good in everybody. Bring out the good in everybody, and never needlessly hurt the feelings of anybody."

Warren's father, George Harding (right), began his career as a farmer. He later became a successful doctor.

HARDING'S CREED

Warren Harding created and posted this set of rules for his *Star* employees to follow as they wrote their news stories. The following are some of his ideas about how journalists should do their work.

The *Star* Office Creed

- Remember there are two sides to every question. Get both.
- Be truthful.
- Get the facts. Mistakes are inevitable, but strive for accuracy. I would rather have one story exactly right then a hundred half wrong.
- Be decent. Be fair. Be generous.
- Boost—don't knock. There's good in everybody. Bring out the good in everybody, and never needlessly hurt the feelings of anybody.
- In reporting a political gathering, get the facts; tell the story as it is, not as you would like to have it.
- Treat all parties alike. If there is any **politics** to be played, we will play it in our **editorial** columns.
- Treat all religious matters reverently.
- If it can possibly be avoided, never bring ignominy to an innocent woman or child in telling the misdeeds or misfortune of a relative. Don't wait to be asked, but do it without asking.
- And, above all, be clean. Never let a dirty word or suggestive story get into type.
- I want this paper so conducted that it can go into any home without destroying the innocence of a child.

CHAPTER TWO

FROM OHIO TO WASHINGTON

Some people say Warren Harding met his future wife, Florence Kling De Wolfe, at the town's roller-skating rink. Others remembered that Florence first saw Warren standing on a street corner. She was so impressed by the handsome newspaperman that she asked a friend to find a way to introduce them. Others say they met when Florence was teaching Warren's younger sister to play piano.

As the owner of the Marion Star, *Harding became well known in his community.*

Florence's father, Amos Kling, was the richest man in town. He had hoped Florence would one day marry a nice young man who would take over his successful businesses. Instead, Florence had endured an unhappy first marriage that ended in divorce. Her father had disapproved of the relationship from the start. After the divorce, he was not very helpful to her.

Florence Kling Harding was stylish, active, and strong-willed.

Florence wasn't meek or gentle, as women were supposed to be in those days. Instead, she was bright, independent, and full of ambition. Since her father wouldn't help her, she decided to earn money by teaching piano. Among her students was one of Warren's younger sisters. Florence loved the Harding family. The house was filled with laughter and warmth. Then she met Warren, who was five years younger than she was. Florence fell in love.

Warren was charming and generous, and his good looks won admirers wherever he went. He had many girlfriends, but Warren noticed something special about Florence. He was pleased that the daughter of Marion's wealthiest citizen liked him. She was bright and interested in learning about his business. He

Warren Harding (center) sits with some of his family members on the front porch of his house in Marion.

still wasn't ready to settle down, but Florence waited patiently. Finally, Warren asked her to marry him. They were married on July 8, 1891.

Florence Harding's father didn't approve of his daughter's new husband. He tried to ruin the *Marion Star* by scaring away its advertisers. He told nasty stories about the Harding family to anyone who would listen. Mrs. Harding did not give up on her husband. If anything, she became more committed to his success.

Shortly after they were married, Florence Harding went to work at the *Star*. She planned to help out for just a few days but ended up working there for 14 years. She took over the **circulation** department. She made sure that customers paid for their **subscriptions** and that newsboys delivered the papers on time. She also took over the advertising department. The Hardings turned the paper into one of most successful in the state.

Warren Harding admired his wife for her education and her strength. He also respected her good business sense. He called her his "Duchess." Harding now concentrated on writing editorials for the paper. The *Marion Star* thrived and soon became the Harding Publishing Company.

Seven years after their marriage, the Duchess and several of their friends suggested that Harding run for a seat in the Ohio Senate. Although Harding did not believe he was cut out for politics, his wife and their friends would not give up. Harding was elected to the senate in 1898 when he was only 33 years old.

Amos Kling was so unhappy about his daughter's marriage to Warren Harding, he refused to attend their wedding. Florence's mother sneaked in to watch the ceremony.

Warren Harding loved the newspaper business. Here, he sits in his office at the Marion Star.

Warren and Florence Harding moved into this house in Marion, Ohio, after their marriage in 1891. It would be their home until 1921.

Harding carried his newspaper's creed into politics. He believed there was good in everybody and immediately won a reputation as an honest man. He was a team player who always went along with the Republican Party policies. When there were disagreements, people counted on Harding to restore peace. Even the Democrats liked him, and they were his party's opponents.

Harding's popularity kept him at the center of the Republican Party. In 1903, Myron T. Herrick became the governor of Ohio. Because of his party loyalty, Harding was rewarded with the job of lieutenant governor. This meant he assisted the governor and would take over if the governor could no longer serve. As lieutenant governor, Harding moved to the state capital, Columbus.

When his term ended in 1905, the Hardings returned to Marion. In 1910, the Republicans chose Harding as their candidate for governor, a race that he lost. Harding was disappointed and vowed never to run for another office. It would not take long for him to break this vow.

A few months before Warren Harding was nominated as the Republican candidate for president, Florence Harding secretly visited a fortuneteller. She asked about the future of a man born on November 2, 1865—her husband's birthday. Later, Mrs. Harding claimed that the fortuneteller told her this man would be a great politician. One day he would be the president. Unfortunately, said the fortuneteller, he would die in office.

Harding's newspaper was known for its fair and evenhanded reporting. This made Harding popular among both Democrats and Republicans.

The Republicans knew Harding was loyal to the party and asked him to run for the U.S. Senate. At first, he refused. But once again, his wife and their political friends changed his mind. After winning the election in 1914, the Hardings moved to Washington, D.C. Florence Harding was thrilled by her new position as the wife of a U.S. senator. Soon the Hardings were friends with some of the wealthiest and most influential people in the nation's capital.

Harding plunged into his work with enthusiasm. When he wasn't on the floor of the Senate, he enjoyed poker parties with old friends from Ohio and new friends he had met in Washington. His wife did not like to gamble, so she acted as the hostess.

Warren Harding (third from right) stands in line with other senators to buy liberty bonds. During World War I, liberty bonds were sold to help pay for the war.

Though Harding was popular in Washington, many politicians did not believe he was cut out to be president. One politician said that Harding's only qualification was that "he looked like a president."

One of his fellow senators said that Harding loved being a senator, but he didn't like all the work and responsibility that went with it. Harding proposed 132 **bills** in his six-year career, but few were of any great importance. Still, he became a notable figure in the Republican Party.

President Woodrow Wilson was too ill in 1920 to seek another term, so the Democrats nominated James Cox. The Republican Party was split between two candidates, General Leonard Wood and Frank O. Lowden. Ohio Republicans named Harding as a candidate as well, but no one expected him to win the nomination. Harding himself wasn't interested in running for president. "The only thing I really worry about," he said, "is that I might be nominated."

Harding's opponent in the presidential election of 1920 was Democrat James Cox. Mr. Cox had a vice-presidential running mate with a bright future. His name was Franklin D. Roosevelt. In 1932, Roosevelt was elected president. He held the office for 12 years—longer than any other president in U.S. history.

Republicans from all over the country gathered in Chicago for their national convention in 1920.

Republican Party leaders met for hours at the Blackstone Hotel to try to settle on a nominee. At two o'clock in the morning, they called in Harding and asked him if he had anything to hide. Harding thought for ten minutes before replying that he did not.

That summer, the Republican Party held its national **convention** in Chicago, Illinois. It took place during one of the worst heat waves in the city's history. Unfortunately, the party couldn't decide between the two favorite candidates. Both of them refused to withdraw from the race. The temperature at the convention hall reached 106 degrees. The **delegates** wanted to make a decision and go home.

Some Republican Party leaders gathered at the nearby Blackstone Hotel to solve the problem. They finally settled on Warren Harding. One senator called him "the best of the second-raters." He meant that if Harding wasn't the party's first choice, he was the best of their second choices.

Harding accepted their decision, saying, "The fates . . . have drawn me into the presidential race." At first, Florence Harding wasn't excited about the prospect. By this time, both she and her husband had serious health problems. She worried that the demands of the presidency would be too much for them. Still, she mustered up the enthusiasm to help her husband **campaign** for office.

One reporter wrote that the decision to nominate Warren Harding had been made "in a smoke-filled room" at the Blackstone Hotel. The phrase "in a smoke-filled room" became a common term for political decisions made in secret.

This campaign button shows Harding and the Republican vice-presidential candidate, Calvin Coolidge.

WOMEN'S SUFFRAGE

Until 1920, women were not allowed to vote in **federal** elections in the United States. The right to vote is called suffrage, and women began fighting for this right in the middle of the 19th century.

Women struggled for more than half a century to gain suffrage. Florence Harding had always supported this quest. She made sure that her husband supported it, too. In 1920—just in time for Warren Harding's presidential campaign—the 19th **Amendment** went into effect, giving women the right to vote in all elections in the United States. This added 25 million new voters to the population. In the photo above, women and men stand in line together to cast votes in 1920.

Both Republicans and Democrats wanted to win women's votes. During the presidential campaign of 1920, Florence Harding was proof of how women could play important roles in business and politics. Many American women respected her ambition and drive. Thanks in large part to her, Warren Harding won a large majority of women's votes.

CHAPTER THREE

A DIFFICULT PRESIDENCY

Instead of touring the country to get votes, Harding used his home in Marion as the campaign headquarters. The American people came to him. Harding called this the "front-porch campaign." Movie stars and entertainers visited the Harding home, as did politicians and business leaders. Marching bands and throngs of ordinary citizens arrived by bus and train from across the country.

The theme of Harding's campaign was "Return to Normalcy." President Woodrow Wilson had led the United States through World War I. Some Americans thought he was cold and distant and didn't care about the American people. He had also been very ill during his last year in office, which worried many citizens. The Hardings convinced voters that they were ordinary people, just like other Americans. People wanted to forget about the hardships of World War I, which had ended in 1918. They wanted a change of leadership. Harding won a **landslide** victory, becoming the 29th president of the United States.

The American people loved the small-town businessman who had become president. In fact, during his term, he was one of the most popular presidents in history. But Harding was aware of his limitations. He surrounded himself with the "best minds" for his **cabinet.** Among these men was a well-known judge named Charles Evans Hughes, Harding's secretary of state. Hughes was in charge of the country's relations with other countries. Future president Herbert Hoover was the secretary of commerce, in charge of business affairs. Financial wizard Andrew Mellon became the secretary of the **treasury.** He was in charge of the government's money.

Woodrow Wilson (left) and Warren Harding ride in a car together on March 4, 1921, the day of Harding's ***inauguration*** *as president.*

Harding and his cabinet are seen here in 1921. As Harding learned more about the ***corruption*** *among his friends and advisers, he began to worry. "I have no trouble with my enemies," he once said. "But my friends. . . . They're the ones that keep me walking the floor nights!"*

Unfortunately, Harding gave other important positions to friends without such strong backgrounds. He named Albert Fall his **secretary of the interior.** He named his campaign manager, Harry Daugherty, the **attorney general.** Harding chose another friend, Charles Forbes, to head the Veteran's Bureau. He would regret these choices later.

President Harding worked hard at his job. He arrived at his desk at eight o'clock every morning, and he often stayed until midnight. But being the president was a difficult job. Harding began to fear that

Harding was very popular during his presidency. Here, supporters gather to shake his hand.

Following World War I, President Wilson proposed the League of Nations, an earlier version of today's United Nations. The league was accepted by all the European powers in 1919, but Republican politicians worked to keep the United States out of it. One month after becoming president, Harding announced that he would not support U.S. membership in the League of Nations.

he could not live up to such responsibility. "I am just beginning to realize what a job I have taken over," said Harding. "God help me, for I need it."

The president did have some successes. He proposed a new government office called the Bureau of the Budget. This bureau was in charge of creating the first formal budget for government spending. A government needs to carefully plan how it will spend its money. Such a plan is called a budget.

Before the new bureau was created, each department in the government handled its own budget. This often resulted in overspending. Creating the bureau saved money. In fact, it helped bring about the first balanced budget in the nation's history. This meant it was the first time the government did not spend more money than it had.

Harding improved relationships with nations that had been enemies of the United States during World War I. He also recognized that the automobile would change the world in the coming years, so he supported the construction of highways around the country. He lowered taxes, pleasing the American people.

In 1921, Harding proposed the Washington Conference for the Limitation of **Armament.** This meeting was meant to control the amount of weapons (arms) that countries could keep. The United States, Great Britain, Japan, France, and Italy all agreed to limit the size of their military forces. Harding delivered the opening speech by remembering the brutality

Warren Harding was the first president to use a microphone and loudspeakers at his inauguration. Before Harding, the new presidents had to shout to be heard.

Harding and many other politicians believed that the United States needed more highways. The country's road system doubled in size during the 1920s.

of World War I: "How can humanity justify, or God forgive? . . . Our hundreds of millions [of people] frankly want less of armament and none of war."

In 1922, Florence Harding brought the first radio into the White House. At the time, the nation had few radio stations. It was an adventure to turn the dial and see what stations could be heard and how far away they were.

During her parties at the White House, Florence Harding used the East Room to show the latest silent movies. Movie stars were frequent guests at the White House.

Harding's social life did not change very much after he became president. Twice-weekly poker parties for Harding's pals were held on the second floor of the White House. He also played golf whenever he could. Florence Harding opened the White House for parties of her own. In fact, she opened the gates to the president's gardens so that the public could wander freely around the grounds. She believed the White House belonged to all Americans, not just the president and his family.

By 1922, Harding's presidency seemed to be going well. But it all soon began to collapse. Both Harding and his wife were still troubled by health problems. To make matters worse, corruption among Harding's cabinet was threatening to destroy his presidency.

One of the worst **scandals** involved Albert Fall, the secretary of the interior. He was caught selling the rights to drill for oil on government lands to private oil companies. The companies paid him thousands of dollars for this right. The money went not to the government, but straight to Fall's bank account. The name of one piece of oil-rich land, Teapot Dome, soon was used to describe the crime, which became known as the Teapot Dome scandal.

Charles Forbes, head of the Veterans Bureau, was arrested for selling government hospital supplies to private companies and keeping the profits for himself.

Harding enjoyed playing golf. As his political life grew more stressful, sports were a way for him to relax.

Harding scolded Forbes in private, but he did not want to tell the public about the crime. Forbes quit his job with the government and left the country. The president hoped the scandal would disappear before Americans learned about it. About two months later, another one of Harding's advisers killed himself. To make matters even worse, there were rumors that the president had a girlfriend. Sick with worry, Harding's health grew steadily weaker.

In 1919, the 18th Amendment to the Constitution made the manufacture and sale of alcoholic beverages against the law. This was called Prohibition. Though Harding voted in favor of Prohibition, the Hardings served alcohol at their private parties. Many people criticized them for supporting Prohibition publicly but refusing to obey the law in private.

LADDIE BOY

During Harding's presidency, an Airedale terrier named Laddie Boy was his constant companion. The dog brought the newspaper to Harding every morning and even sat in on cabinet meetings in a special chair. When the president practiced golf on the White House lawn, Laddie Boy fetched the balls, scooping them up in his mouth and returning them for Harding's next shot. Newspaper columns were written about the dog. Many Americans wanted a pet just like the president's. A company named a canned food after him, and there was even a child's stuffed Laddie Boy toy.

At the dinner table in the White House dining room, Harding would offer treats from his plate to Laddie Boy. Mrs. Harding would tell the president to stop feeding the dog. Laddie Boy would then journey to her end of the table, where Mrs. Harding would feed him from her plate.

When the Hardings quarreled and refused to speak to each other, they sometimes brought the poor dog into the arguments: "Laddie, tell the Duchess she's 100-percent wrong!"

CHAPTER FOUR

JOURNEY TO DISASTER

Harding was troubled by the corruption in his **administration.** It hurt him that people he believed were his friends had committed crimes. Harding wondered what to do. He asked his secretary of commerce, Herbert Hoover, for advice. Hoover suggested that Harding tell newspaper reporters what he knew. At least that way, the American people would still believe that their president was an honest man.

Harding's presidency was brief and troubled.

Harding was afraid, so he didn't talk to reporters. He instead decided it was a good time to leave Washington. Harding planned a cross-country trip that would take him all the way to Alaska. Along the way, he would meet the American people and give many speeches. He

When Harding visited Vancouver during his "Voyage of Understanding," he became the first U.S. president to visit Canada.

called this trip the "Voyage of Understanding" because he planned to listen to the ideas and concerns of the nations' citizens.

President Harding was still ill. His blood pressure was high, and he often couldn't catch his breath. Just in case something should go wrong, the Hardings brought their doctor along for the journey. The president's train departed Washington on June 20, 1923.

The trip was a huge success, but the long journey was difficult for Harding. After reaching Alaska, the president's party took a boat down the West Coast to San Francisco, California. Along the way, Harding was struck by severe stomach problems. By the time he reached the Palace Hotel in San Francisco, he had grown very weak.

Florence Harding (buckling helmet) was the first president's wife to fly in an airplane. She was fitted with goggles, pants, and a helmet and then took off for a 30-minute flight. A female pilot flew the plane.

Alaska governor Scott C. Bone wore a fur-lined coat when President and Mrs. Harding visited him in Anchorage. Harding's visit to Alaska was the first ever by a president.

On August 2, Florence Harding was reading to the president. Suddenly, he turned pale, saying he felt strange. Slowly, the color returned to his face, and Mrs. Harding continued to read. A few moments later, at 7:35 in the evening, Warren Harding died. The cause of his death was probably a heart attack. Vice President Calvin Coolidge was sworn in as president early the next morning.

In the months before he died, Harding had been battling with American steel companies to make them shorten their workdays from 12 hours to 8 hours. After his death, the companies lowered their workdays to 8 hours in his honor.

Americans were struck with grief over Harding's death. Mourners lined the tracks as the train bearing Harding's body returned to Washington. His body lay in the White House East Room overnight. Florence Harding spent two hours sitting next to his casket talking to him. His body was then transferred to the

When Harding died, Vice President Calvin Coolidge became president. Here, Coolidge and his wife, Grace, leave the Capitol after viewing Harding's casket.

After Harding's death, newspaper delivery boys from across the country sent 19,342 pennies to a special fund. These coins were melted down and made into a statue of Laddie Boy. The statue now belongs to the Smithsonian Institution in Washington, D.C.

Capitol, where thousands came to pay their respects. Finally, a train took Harding's remains back to Marion, Ohio, where he was buried. The president's widow died just 15 months later.

Unfortunately, news of the corruption in his administration began to reach the public after Harding's death. Stories about his relationships with other women were reported in books and papers. A few people even claimed that Mrs. Harding had murdered the president. She had refused to allow an **autopsy** on his body, which would have confirmed the cause of his death. Some people said she did this because she had killed him. New scandals also surfaced, including the Teapot Dome scandal. The president himself was not proven guilty of wrongdoing, but his good name suffered. The man who had been such a popular president quickly became known as a terrible leader. After all, it was his closest political friends who were guilty of the crimes.

In every list ranking the presidents from best to worst, Harding is at the bottom. But during his lifetime, the American people loved him. Perhaps his biggest failure was that he did not reveal the corruption and try to stop it. "I cannot hope to be one of the greatest presidents," Harding once said, "but perhaps I can be remembered as one of the best loved." But even this was not to be. As much as Harding tried to be a good man, his presidency is remembered for its corruption.

President Harding was good-natured and well-liked, but he was not a strong leader. Most experts consider him one of the nation's weakest presidents.

HOMEOPATHIC MEDICINE

Warren Harding's father, George (below right), practiced **homeopathic** medicine. Homeopathic doctors believe that they can cure an illness by giving tiny doses of something that produces the same symptoms as the illness. How did George Harding treat a common cold? He made a medicine out of onions because they make the eyes water and the nose run.

Long after George Harding retired, Florence and Warren Harding continued to believe in homeopathic medicine. They went to Charles "Doc" Sawyer with any health problems they had. Sawyer created his own homeopathic hospital on a farm outside of Marion, Ohio. Sawyer's cures included vigorous exercise and massage. He took X-rays of the skull to find any "bony lumps" that might affect the brain. His patients also took whirlpool baths and doses of medicine made from plants.

Florence Harding had great trust in Sawyer's treatments. Sawyer even traveled with the Hardings to Alaska during the "Voyage of Understanding." In the photo above, Sawyer (in background) watches as President Harding leaves a train in San Francisco shortly before his death.

The president became ill with stomach problems just before he died, probably because of crabs he had eaten. Sawyer used medicine that caused Harding to urinate frequently, claiming it would remove **"toxins"** from the body. Other doctors believed this treatment did more harm than good. They claimed the treatment might even have weakened Harding's heart, leading to a heart attack. No one knows for sure what caused Harding's death because an autopsy was never performed. But Florence Harding stood by Doc Sawyer to the end.

TIME LINE

1860 | 1870 | 1880 | 1890 | 1900

1865
Warren Harding is born on November 2 in Corsica (now Blooming Grove), Ohio. His parents are George Tryon and Phoebe Dickerson Harding.

1873
The Harding family moves to Caledonia, Ohio, where George works as a homeopathic doctor. Phoebe earns money as a midwife. Warren takes his first job at the *Caledonia Argus* as a printer's devil.

1879
Harding enters Ohio Central College, where he edits the school newspaper and joins a band.

1882
Harding's family moves to Marion, Ohio. He takes a job at the weekly paper, the *Marion Democratic Mirror*.

1884
Harding and two friends buy the *Marion Star*, a weekly newspaper. They publish their first edition on November 26.

1891
On July 8, Harding marries Florence Kling De Wolfe. She is five years older than he. Her father, Amos Kling, is the richest man in town. Kling objects to the marriage and refuses to attend the wedding.

1898
On November 6, Harding is elected an Ohio state senator. He meets Harry Daugherty, who will become a close political ally.

1903
Rewarded by the Republican Party for his loyalty, Harding is elected lieutenant governor of Ohio.

1910 1920

1910
Harding is defeated as the Republican candidate for governor.

1914
Harding is elected to the U.S. Senate.

1917
Senator Harding votes in favor of Prohibition, which makes the manufacture and sale of alcohol illegal in the United States.

1919
Harding votes in favor of women's suffrage. Prohibition becomes law when the 18th Amendment to the Constitution is approved.

1920
When the 19th Amendment is approved, all American women are allowed to vote in national elections for the first time. Republicans choose Harding to be their presidential candidate at their national convention in Chicago. Harding runs a "front-porch" campaign, speaking to supporters from his Marion, Ohio, home. He is elected president on November 2.

1921
Harding is inaugurated on March 4. He creates a cabinet made up of "great minds and old friends." Many of the "old friends" will later cause problems within his administration. Harding signs an act establishing the Bureau of the Budget. Harding helps create the Washington Conference for the Limitation of Armament.

1922
Albert Fall, Harding's secretary of the interior, takes bribes to lease oil reserves on government land to private oil companies. Harding makes the first presidential radio broadcast on June 14. He is the first president to speak on the radio.

1923
Charles Forbes, the head of the Veterans Bureau, is accused of stealing hospital supplies and taking money from construction companies. On June 20, the Hardings begin a train trip across the country to Alaska, which the president calls his "Voyage of Understanding." The president delivers more than 80 speeches along the way. On July 26, Harding becomes the first president to visit Canada when he gives a speech in Vancouver, British Columbia. On July 28, Harding becomes ill from what his doctor calls food poisoning. On August 2, Warren Harding dies, probably from a heart attack. He is 57 years old. The next day, Vice President Calvin Coolidge is sworn in as president.

1924
Florence Harding dies on November 21.

GLOSSARY

administration (ad-min-uh-STRAY-shun) An administration is the group of people who are in charge of running the U.S. government. The president and his cabinet are the administration.

amendment (uh-MEND-munt) An amendment is a change or addition made to the Constitution or other documents. The 19th Amendment gave American women the right to vote.

armament (AR-muh-munt) Armament is weapons and other equipment used by the military. Harding called a conference to reduce armament in countries around the world.

attorney general (uh-TUR-nee JEN-rul) The attorney general is the chief lawyer of the country. Harding named Harry Daugherty the attorney general.

autopsy (AH-top-see) An autopsy is a medical examination of a dead body usually done to determine the cause of death. An autopsy was never performed on Harding's body.

bills (BILZ) Bills are ideas for new laws that are presented to a group of lawmakers. Harding proposed 132 bills during his time as a senator.

cabinet (KAB-nit) A cabinet is the group of people who advise a president. Harding chose many respected people for his cabinet.

campaign (kam-PAYN) A campaign is the process of running for an election, including activities such as giving speeches or attending rallies. Harding ran his campaign from his home in Ohio.

candidate (KAN-duh-dayt) A candidate is a person running in an election. The Republicans chose Harding as their candidate for governor in 1910.

circulation (sur-kyoo-LAY-shun) A newspaper's circulation is the number of copies it sells. Florence Harding took over the circulation department at the *Marion Star* and was in charge of making sure all the papers were delivered and paid for.

convention (kun-VEN-shun) A convention is a meeting. The Democratic and Republican political parties hold national conventions every four years to choose their presidential candidates.

corruption (kuh-RUP-shun) Corruption is dishonesty. Harding's friends were accused of corruption.

creed (KREED) A creed is a statement of beliefs by which to live. Harding created a creed for his employees at the *Marion Star* to follow.

delegates (DEL-uh-gitz) Delegates are people elected to take part in something. Delegates at the Republican National Convention chose Harding as their 1920 presidential candidate.

Democrat (DEM-uh-krat) A Democrat is a person who belongs to the Democratic political party. Harding defeated Democrat James Cox to become president.

editorial (ed-ih-TOR-ee-ul) An editorial is an article that gives the opinion of the editor or publisher of a newspaper. Warren Harding wrote editorials for the *Marion Star*.

federal (FED-ur-ul) Federal refers to the national government of the United States, rather than a state or city government. Women could not vote in federal elections until 1920.

homeopathic (hom-ee-oh-PATH-ik) Homeopathic medicine treats an illness with small doses of medicine that produce symptoms of the illness. George Harding was a homeopathic doctor.

inauguration (ih-nawg-yuh-RAY-shun) An inauguration is the ceremony that takes place when a new president begins a term. Harding was the first president to use a microphone at his inauguration.

journalism (JER-nul-iz-um) Journalism is the work of gathering, writing, and presenting true stories for newspapers, magazines, TV, and radio. Harding liked the idea of working in journalism and seeing his words in print.

landslide (LAND-slyde) If a candidate wins an election by a landslide, he or she wins by a huge number of votes. Harding won the 1920 presidential election by a landslide.

nominated (NOM-ih-nayt-ed) If a political party nominated someone, it chose him or her to run for a political office. Harding worried that he might be nominated as the Republican presidential candidate.

political parties (puh-LIT-uh-kul PAR-teez) Political parties are groups of people who share similar ideas about how to run a government. People from opposing political parties often have differences of opinion.

politics (PAWL-uh-tiks) Politics refers to the actions and practices of the government. Harding did not think he was cut out for a life in politics.

rally (RAL-ee) A rally is an organized gathering of people to show support for something or someone. Harding went to a Republican rally in 1884 to support a candidate.

Republicans (ri-PUB-lih-kunz) Republicans are people who belong to the Republican political party. Harding and his family were Republicans.

scandals (SKAN-dulz) Scandals are shameful actions that shock the public. Harding hoped the scandals involving his friends would disappear before Americans found out about them.

secretary of the interior (SEK-ruh-tayr-ee OF THE in-TEER-ee-ur) The secretary of the interior is a member of the president's cabinet. He or she heads the department in charge of how U.S. land is used.

sensational (sen-SAY-shun-ul) If a newspaper article is sensational, it is meant to stir up strong feelings in its readers. Harding hated sensational stories filled with crime, tragedy, and misfortune.

subscriptions (sub-SKRIP-shunz) Subscriptions are arrangements where people prepay for a certain number of issues of a newspaper or magazine. Florence Harding made sure that customers paid for their subscriptions.

toxins (TOK-sinz) Toxins are poisons that have a bad effect on human health. A doctor thought that crabs Harding ate had infected the president's body with toxins.

treasury (TREZH-ur-ee) A treasury manages the flow of money in a government, including its income and expenses. Andrew Mellon was Harding's secretary of the treasury.

THE UNITED STATES GOVERNMENT

The United States government is divided into three equal branches: the executive, the legislative, and the judicial. This division helps prevent abuses of power because each branch has to answer to the other two. No one branch can become too powerful.

EXECUTIVE BRANCH

President
Vice President
Departments

The job of the executive branch is to enforce the laws. It is headed by the president, who serves as the spokesperson for the United States around the world. The president signs bills into law and appoints important officials such as federal judges. He or she is also the commander in chief of the U.S. military. The president is assisted by the vice president, who takes over if the president dies or cannot carry out the duties of the office.

The executive branch also includes various departments, each focused on a specific topic. They include the Defense Department, the Justice Department, and the Agriculture Department. The department heads, along with other officials such as the vice president, serve as the president's closest advisers, called the cabinet.

LEGISLATIVE BRANCH

Congress
Senate and
House of Representatives

The job of the legislative branch is to make the laws. It consists of Congress, which is divided into two parts: the Senate and the House of Representatives. The Senate has 100 members, and the House of Representatives has 435 members. Each state has two senators. The number of representatives a state has varies depending on the state's population.

Besides making laws, Congress also passes budgets and enacts taxes. In addition, it is responsible for declaring war, maintaining the military, and regulating trade with other countries.

JUDICIAL BRANCH

Supreme Court
Courts of Appeals
District Courts

The job of the judicial branch is to interpret the laws. It consists of the nation's federal courts. Trials are held in district courts. During trials, judges must decide what laws mean and how they apply. Courts of appeals review the decisions made in district courts.

The nation's highest court is the Supreme Court. If someone disagrees with a court of appeals ruling, he or she can ask the Supreme Court to review it. The Supreme Court may refuse. The Supreme Court makes sure that decisions and laws do not violate the Constitution.

CHOOSING THE PRESIDENT

It may seem odd, but American voters don't elect the president directly. Instead, the president is chosen using what is called the Electoral College.

Each state gets as many votes in the Electoral College as its combined total of senators and representatives in Congress. For example, Iowa has two senators and five representatives, so it gets seven electoral votes. Although the District of Columbia does not have any voting members in Congress, it gets three electoral votes. Usually, the candidate who wins the most votes in any given state receives all of that state's electoral votes.

To become president, a candidate must get more than half of the Electoral College votes. There are a total of 538 votes in the Electoral College, so a candidate needs 270 votes to win. If nobody receives 270 Electoral College votes, the House of Representatives chooses the president.

With the Electoral College system, the person who receives the most votes nationwide does not always receive the most electoral votes. This happened most recently in 2000, when Al Gore received half a million more national votes than George W. Bush. Bush became president because he had more Electoral College votes.

THE WHITE HOUSE

The White House is the official home of the president of the United States. It is located at 1600 Pennsylvania Avenue NW in Washington, D.C. In 1792, a contest was held to select the architect who would design the president's home. James Hoban won. Construction took eight years.

The first president, George Washington, never lived in the White House. The second president, John Adams, moved into the house in 1800, though the inside was not yet complete. During the War of 1812, British soldiers burned down much of the White House. It was rebuilt several years later.

The White House was changed through the years. Porches were added, and President Theodore Roosevelt added the West Wing. President William Taft changed the shape of the presidential office, making it into the famous Oval Office. While Harry Truman was president, the old house was discovered to be structurally weak. All the walls were reinforced with steel, and the rooms were rebuilt.

Today, the White House has 132 rooms (including 35 bathrooms), 28 fireplaces, and 3 elevators. It takes 570 gallons of paint to cover the outside of the six-story building. The White House provides the president with many ways to relax. It includes a putting green, a jogging track, a swimming pool, a tennis court, and beautifully landscaped gardens. The White House also has a movie theater, a billiard room, and a one-lane bowling alley.

PRESIDENTIAL PERKS

The job of president of the United States is challenging. It is probably one of the most stressful jobs in the world. Because of this, presidents are paid well, though not nearly as well as the leaders of large corporations. In 2007, the president earned $400,000 a year. Presidents also receive extra benefits that make the demanding job a little more appealing.

★ **Camp David:** In the 1940s, President Franklin D. Roosevelt chose this heavily wooded spot in the mountains of Maryland to be the presidential retreat, where presidents can relax. Even though it is a retreat, world business is conducted there. Most famously, President Jimmy Carter met with Middle Eastern leaders at Camp David in 1978. The result was a peace agreement between Israel and Egypt.

★ ***Air Force One*:** The president flies on a jet called *Air Force One*. It is a Boeing 747-200B that has been modified to meet the president's needs. *Air Force One* is the size of a large home. It is equipped with a dining room, sleeping quarters, a conference room, and office space. It also has two kitchens that can provide food for up to 50 people.

★ **The Secret Service:** While not the most glamorous of the president's perks, the Secret Service is one of the most important. The Secret Service is a group of highly trained agents who protect the president and the president's family.

★ **The Presidential State Car:** The presidential limousine is a stretch Cadillac DTS. It has been armored to protect the president in case of attack. Inside the plush car are a foldaway desk, an entertainment center, and a communications console.

★ **The Food:** The White House has five chefs who will make any food the president wants. The White House also has an extensive wine collection.

★ **Retirement:** A former president receives a pension, or retirement pay, of just under $180,000 a year. Former presidents also receive Secret Service protection for the rest of their lives.

FACTS

Qualifications

To run for president, a candidate must

- ★ be at least 35 years old
- ★ be a citizen who was born in the United States
- ★ have lived in the United States for 14 years

Term of Office

A president's term of office is four years.
No president can stay in office for more than two terms.

Election Date

The presidential election takes place every four years on the first Tuesday of November.

Inauguration Date

Presidents are inaugurated on January 20.

Oath of Office

I do solemnly swear I will faithfully execute the office of the President of the United States and will to the best of my ability preserve, protect, and defend the Constitution of the United States.

Write a Letter to the President

One of the best things about being a U.S. citizen is that Americans get to participate in their government. They can speak out if they feel government leaders aren't doing their jobs. They can also praise leaders who are going the extra mile. Do you have something you'd like the president to do? Should the president worry more about the environment and encourage people to recycle? Should the government spend more money on our schools? You can write a letter to the president to say how you feel!

1600 Pennsylvania Avenue
Washington, D.C. 20500
You can even send an e-mail to: president@whitehouse.gov

Books

Kent, Deborah. *Warren G. Harding: America's 29th President.* New York: Children's Press, 2004.

Orr, Tamra B. *Prohibition.* San Diego: Blackbirch Press, 2004.

Rossi, Ann. *Votes for Women.* Washington, DC: National Geographic, 2003.

Somervill, Barbara A. *Warren G. Harding.* Minneapolis: Compass Point, 2004.

Thorndike, Jonathan L. *The Teapot Dome Scandal Trial: A Headline Court Case.* Berkeley Heights, NJ: Enslow Publishers, 2001.

Videos

The History Channel Presents The Presidents. DVD (New York: A&E Home Video, 2005).

National Geographic's Inside the White House. DVD (Washington, DC: National Geographic Video, 2003).

Internet Sites

Visit our Web page for lots of links about Warren G. Harding and other U.S. presidents:

http://www.childsworld.com/links

Note to Parents, Teachers, and Librarians: We routinely verify our Web links to make sure they are safe, active sites—so encourage your readers to check them out!

INDEX